VIRTUAL BANALITY

VIRTUAL BANALITY

A FUSCO BROTHERS COLLECTION

by J.C. Duffy

Andrews and McMeel
A Universal Press Syndicate Company
Kansas City

5

YOU KNOW, RÖLF, I THINK I ONLY LOOK SHORT NEXT TO YOU BECAUSE YOU'RE HIGH-WAISTED...IT'S AN OPTICAL ILLUSION.

BUS

I ONLY SEEM HIGH-WAISTED TO YOU BECAUSE YOU ARE SHORT, AXEL...

ACTUALLY, I SEEM LOW-WAISTED TO MOST PEOPLE.

WHY WOULD THAT BE??

BECAUSE I'M SO HIGH-MINDED.

YOU KNOW, GLORIA, YOU REALLY MAKE MY MIND SORE.

I MAKE YOUR MIND SOAR, OR I MAKE YOUR MIND SORE??

YES.

WE'LL TALK ABOUT THIS WHEN YOU GET HERE, LANCE.

SHE HATES IT WHEN SHE CAN'T SEE THE SPELLING IN MY WORD BALLOONS OVER THE PHONE.

CLICK.

YOU KNOW WHAT YOUR PROBLEM IS, RÖLF? YOUR BRAIN DOESN'T SPEND ENOUGH TIME LIVING IN THE TOP HALF OF YOUR BODY...

WHICH IS, AFTER ALL, WHERE NATURE PUT IT IN THE FIRST PLACE.

MY BRAIN USUALLY LIVES IN THE TOP PART OF MY BODY, VERONICA— I JUST THOUGHT IT SEEMED LIKE SUCH A SPECIAL NIGHT, I'D LET IT SEE HOW THE OTHER HALF LIVES.

"KEEP YOUR FEET ON THE GROUND, AND KEEP REACHING FOR THE STARS." -CASEY KASEM

8

13

14

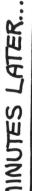

MINUTES LATER...

A CONTROVERSIAL NEW LOOK AT THE CHARACTER ASSASSINATION OF LANCE FUSCO...

AXEL, DO YOU REALIZE THAT 90 PERCENT OF AMERICAN STUDENTS SCORE BELOW THE INTERNATIONAL AVERAGE, SCHOLASTICALLY?!? AND WHY?? IT'S BECAUSE THEY WATCH THE MOST TELEVISION!!!

GEE, RÖLF, I GUESS THAT'S SOMETHING I SHOULD REALLY THINK ABOUT...WHERE DID YOU READ THAT?

I SAW IT ON TV.

I THINK I'M DEPRESSED BECAUSE I'M GETTING CLOSER AND CLOSER TO 30, AL...

LOOK ON THE BRIGHT SIDE, WENDY...IN A FEW YEARS YOU'LL BE GETTING FARTHER AND FARTHER AWAY FROM 30.

THAT'S EITHER INCREDIBLY STUPID OR INCREDIBLY INSIGHTFUL...I CAN'T FIGURE OUT WHICH.

THAT'S GOOD.

WHY CAN'T I GO WITH YOU TO THE STAR TREK CONVENTION, AL?

BECAUSE YOU CAN'T MAKE THE VULCAN "LIVE LONG AND PROSPER" SIGN WITH YOUR PAW, AXEL.

STAR TREK THE SNACK

MAYBE THIS WILL DO: IT'S A KLINGON SIGN...

FOR "LIVE LONG AND PROSPER"?

FOR "DROP DEAD AND FESTER".

26

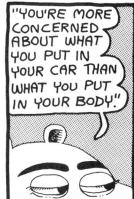

WHAT'S FOR DINNER, AL? I'M STARVED!

BLACKENED CHICKEN.

HMM...WHAT ELSE?

BLACKENED RICE.

I SEE...

MAYBE I'LL JUST HAVE SOME BLACKENED COFFEE.

I THOUGHT WE MIGHT TRY SOMETHING DIFFERENT, LANCE... YOU'VE HEARD OF CLARIFIED BUTTER?

YES...

CLARIFIED COFFEE.

I FEEL I SHOULD WARN YOU, DANA — I'VE BEEN TOLD I HAVE AN ADDICTIVE PERSONALITY...

GEE, THANKS FOR BEING CANDID, RÖLF...DID A PSYCHIATRIST TELL YOU THIS?

NO, IT'S THE CONSENSUS OF THE WOMEN I'VE DATED...ONE TASTE OF MY PERSONALITY AND YOU'RE ADDICTED.

DON'T YOU EVER GET TIRED OF READING THAT TURGID PULP, AL? HOW DO YOU EXPECT TO LEARN ANYTHING?

PROUST

TURGID PULP

PULP IS FINE, AXEL, AS LONG AS IT RETAINS ITS...ITS... IS IT "TURGIDNESS" OR "TURGIDITY"?

GEE, I DON'T KNOW...

FUNNY THING...YOU TAKE THE HIGH ROAD AND I'LL TAKE THE LOW ROAD, AND WE'LL BOTH ARRIVE STUPID.

32

34

NIRVANA

OPEN

OOH! LET'S GO INTO THIS NEW AGE SHOP, LANCE!!

I DON'T KNOW IF I CAN HANDLE SHOPPING IN A NEW AGE SHOP, GLORIA.

HOW ABOUT IF I HANDLE THE SHOPPING PART, AND YOU HANDLE THE AGING PART?

CAN DO.

WOW, GLORIA— LOOK AT ALL THESE SHOES! I'M VERY IMPRESSED!!

I GUESS IT IS KIND OF IMPRESSIVE THAT A LOT OF PEOPLE LEAVE THEIR SHOES AT THE DOOR IN A NEW AGE SHOP, LANCE... I SUPPOSE IT'S BECAUSE THEY SELL SUCH SPIRITUAL PRODUCTS HERE.

OH...I THOUGHT THEY JUST DESCENDED DIRECTLY INTO HEAVEN... I'M NO LONGER IMPRESSED.

I JUST LOVE BROWSING IN THESE NEW AGE SHOPS, LANCE!!

MMM.

TAROT CARDS, PYRAMIDS, CRYSTALS, ASTRO-DICE, HEART WANDS... IT'S ALL SO SPIRITUAL!!

OH, LOOK, GLORIA—RIGHT BETWEEN THE INCENSE AND THE SACRED PATH CARDS—IT'S SOME KIND OF SPECIAL SPIRITUAL CAMERA!!

IT PROBABLY LOOKS DIRECTLY INTO YOUR SOUL!! AMAZING!!!

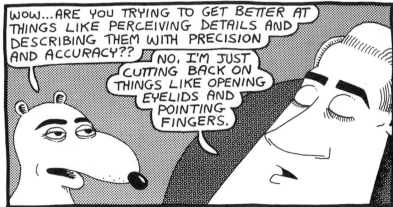

STAY TUNED FOR A VERY SPECIAL "FUSCO BROTHERS"...

NEXT ON THIS PAGE.

GIVE IT TO ME STRAIGHT, DOC.

VERY WELL, MR. FUSCO...YOU'RE LACTOSE-INTOL-ERANT.

OH, MY GOD!!!

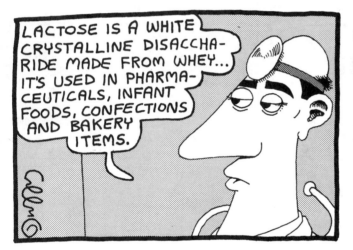

LACTOSE IS A WHITE CRYSTALLINE DISACCHA-RIDE MADE FROM WHEY... IT'S USED IN PHARMA-CEUTICALS, INFANT FOODS, CONFECTIONS AND BAKERY ITEMS.

I KNEW THAT... WHAT DOES "INTOLERANT" MEAN?

ALL THIS MEANS IS THAT YOU'LL NEED TO TAKE SOME OVER-THE-COUNTER PRODUCTS TO HELP YOU DIGEST YOUR JELLY DOUGHNUTS FROM NOW ON...

RELAX!

NOTHING DAMPENS SECOND-CHANCE-AT-LIFE EUPHORIA FASTER THAN FALLING INTO AN OPEN MANHOLE.

CLICK!

40

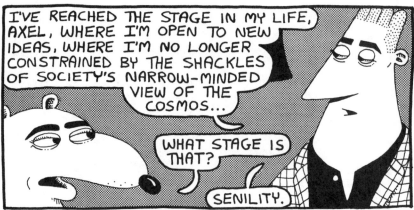

ANOTHER RENT INCREASE?!!?

!!#%©?✱!!

EASY ON THE LANGUAGE, LANCE...AFTER ALL, I'M AN IMPRESSIONABLE YOUNGSTER.

I BEG YOUR PARDON, AXEL... HOW ABOUT IF I CALMLY MENTION THAT I THINK OUR LANDLORD IS A PAIN IN THE ANKLE, AND JUST INTERNALIZE MY RAGE IN THE FORM OF AN ULCER?

I'D APPRECIATE IT.

HAS IT REALLY BEEN A YEAR SINCE OUR LAST RENT INCREASE?

YOU WOULD HAVE THAT INFORMATION AT YOUR FINGERTIPS IF YOU HAD MADE A NOTE OF IT IN YOUR TWO-YEAR PLANNER, LANCE.

TWO-YEAR PLANNER?? MY ABILITY TO PLAN AHEAD DOESN'T EXTEND QUITE THAT FAR, AXEL.

HOW FAR DOES IT EXTEND?

TO THE SNOOZE BUTTON ON MY ALARM CLOCK.

THAT'S AN INTERESTING COLOGNE YOU'RE WEARING... WHAT'S IT CALLED?

"NEW CAR SCENT"...MOST GUYS JUST SPRAY IT IN THEIR CARS, BUT I LIKE A LITTLE BEHIND MY EARS.

FASCINATING...IS IT EFFECTIVE??

IT'S MORE EFFECTIVE THAN "PUBLIC TRANSPORTATION SCENT," BUT LESS EFFECTIVE THAN "U.S. TREASURY SCENT."

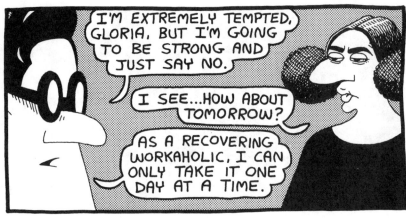

COULD I BORROW YOUR LIPSTICK FOR A MOMENT, GLORIA?

UH...SURE, AL... WHAT FOR?

I FIGURE IF I GO OUT WITH LIPSTICK ON MY CHEEK, SOME WOMAN WILL SEE IT AND WANT TO GET SOME OF WHAT I'VE GOT...

BECAUSE WHAT I'VE GOT MUST BE HOT...

BECAUSE SOME OTHER WOMAN IS GETTING WHAT I'VE GOT, SO WHAT I'VE GOT MUST BE WORTH GETTING... GET IT??

I DIDN'T KNOW PRICKLY HEAT WAS A HOT COMMODITY ON THE DATING SCENE THESE DAYS, AL.

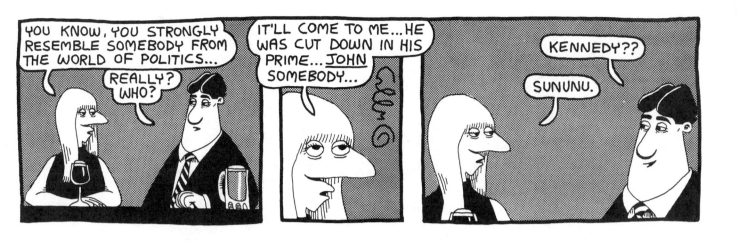

50

51

HMM...I CAN WATCH "MATLOCK" FROM NEW YORK, OR I CAN WATCH "MATLOCK" FROM ATLANTA... SO MANY OPTIONS!!

YOU KNOW, AL, MAYBE INSTEAD OF SITTING HERE WATCHING RERUNS, YOU SHOULD GET A LIFE.

I THOUGHT HAVING CABLE WAS CONSIDERED HAVING A LIFE, AXEL...

NOT EXACTLY.

WOW...

BOY, IT'S A GOOD THING I'M SITTING DOWN, AS THIS IS QUITE A SHOCKER...MAYBE I SHOULD SPEND MOST OF MY TIME SITTING DOWN FROM NOW ON, AS A PRECAUTION.

YOU'VE GOT A LIFE, LANCE— WHAT'S YOUR ADVICE?

IT'S NOT ALL IT'S CRACKED UP TO BE, AL...GET PAY-PER-VIEW.

LOVE IS LIKE A BIG ROCK, AL, ROLLING DOWN A STEEP HILL...

ONCE IT STARTS ROLLING, IT'S IMPOSSIBLE TO STOP.

MAYBE YOU SHOULD TRY IT ON A FLAT SURFACE SOMETIME.

!!!

I THINK THE PROBLEM IS THAT WE'RE JUST VERY DIFFERENT, LANCE...

PSYCHOLOGY TODAY

ASTEROID RESEMBLING HUGH DOWNS HURTLING TOWARD EARTH

WILD NEWS

ARE YOU SAYING WE'RE SEPARATE AND DISTINCT, OR VARIOUS AND ASSORTED, OR DISSIMILAR TO EACH OTHER, OR UNLIKE OTHER PEOPLE, OR WHAT, GLORIA?

I'M SAYING I'M NORMAL AND YOU'RE OUT OF YOUR MIND.

THAT CLEARS _THAT_ UP.

JOB-HUNTING, AL??

JUST BROWSING, AXEL.

CLASSIFIED

MAYBE YOU SHOULD FIND OUT WHERE YOUR STRONG SUIT LIES BEFORE YOU GO ON ANY INTERVIEWS.

I ALREADY KNOW WHERE MY STRONG SUIT LIES.

WHERE?

IT LIES AT THE DRY CLEANER'S... IT WAS GETTING A LITTLE _TOO_ STRONG.

HI, MY NAME IS LARS... MAY I SIT HERE?

I HAVE AN IRON-CLAD RULE...

YOU DON'T TALK TO STRANGERS IN THE PARK?

NO, I HAVE AN ACTUAL IRON-CLAD RULE!!

I HAVE TO BE JOGGING OFF NOW.

DO YOU ENGAGE IN MUCH OUTDOOR RECREATIONAL ACTIVITY, RÖLF?

NOT REALLY.

IT SHOWS... PERSONALLY, I'M A HORSE-WOMAN.

I DON'T THINK YOU SHOULD LET YOUR LOOKS PREVENT YOU FROM GOING OUTSIDE, AGNES...AND ANYWAY, I THINK YOU'RE BEING OVERLY SELF-CRITICAL.

YOU'RE READING PROUST, AL?

I DECIDED THAT THE BEST WAY TO GET MYSELF TO IMPROVE MY MIND WAS TO TAKE A PAGE OUT OF GEORGE BUSH'S BOOK AND GIVE THE PROJECT A CATCHY NAME THAT I COULD RALLY BEHIND...

REALLY??

WHAT NAME?

NO, RALLY...

"OPERATION DESERT BRAIN."

NEWSTIME

PROUST

56

YOU'RE LATE, LANCE...I HOPE YOU HAVE A GOOD EXCUSE THIS TIME.

I GOT FOGGED IN, GLORIA.

FOGGED IN?? ARE YOU TELLING ME YOU JUST FLEW IN FROM OUT OF TOWN???

I'M TELLING YOU THAT AFTER WATCHING OPRAH, PHIL, SALLY JESSY, MAURY AND GERALDO ALL DAY, ANYBODY WOULD FEEL FOGGED IN.

DO WE HAVE ANY FAMILY SECRETS, LANCE?

FAMILY ALBUM

NEWSTIME

HMM...WELL, YOU ALREADY KNOW YOU'RE ADOPTED, SO I CAN'T SHATTER YOUR WORLD WITH THAT ONE...

SORRY.

DOES THE FACT THAT I KEEP SECRET THE FACT THAT I HAVE A FAMILY COUNT AS A FAMILY SECRET?

I'LL GET BACK TO YOU ON THAT ONE.

HOW WAS YOUR DATE, AL?

SHE TOLD ME ONE RIVETING STORY AFTER ANOTHER, LARS...

GEE, THAT'S GREAT...I GUESS THAT MEANS YOU'LL BE GOING OUT WITH HER AGAIN.

AU CONTRAIRE... IT'S THE LAST TIME I GO OUT WITH A RIVETER!!!

DING DONG

HI, I'M TED WIENER, YOUR YUPPIE NEIGHBOR FROM DOWN THE STREET... REMEMBER ME?

VAGUELY.

IF YOU RECALL, AS BLOCK CAPTAIN, I STOPPED BY LAST YEAR TO POINT OUT THAT NO ONE FROM THIS HOUSE HAD ATTENDED A BLOCK MEETING SINCE WE STOPPED SERVING WINE AND CHEESE...

SOUNDS PRETTY FAR-FETCHED SO FAR, BUT GO ON.

WELL, I'M PLEASED TO ANNOUNCE THAT AT TONIGHT'S MEETING WE'LL BE SERVING WINE, CHEESE, AND ZUCCHINI STICKS IN A ZESTY RANCHERO SAUCE...

ANY QUESTIONS?

DO YOU DELIVER?

RÖLF, DO STALAGMITES GROW UP, OR DOWN?

YES.

AND IF THAT ANSWER ISN'T SPECIFIC ENOUGH, YOUR TEACHER CAN COME AND SPEAK TO ME PERSONALLY.

FINE.

WAIT A MINUTE...IS THIS FOR THAT ATTRACTIVE MS. FENWICK, OR THAT BURLY MR. JOHNSON??

YES.

HEY...WHAT HAPPENED TO THE CARPET, LARS??

I THREW IT OUT, RÖLF...I FIGURED IT WOULD BE EASIER TO SPOT THE BUGS IF THEY WEREN'T CAMOUFLAGED.

YOU KNOW, I WAS HOPING THAT AT SOME POINT WE'D GO FROM RAGS TO RICHES, INSTEAD OF FROM RUGS TO ROACHES....

LANCE, WHY DO YOU HAVE DIFFICULTY SHARING YOUR INNERMOST FEARS, HANG-UPS, AND ANXIETIES WITH ME?

I DON'T WANT TO SUBMIT MYSELF TO YOUR ARMCHAIR ANALYSIS, GLORIA.

IT WOULDN'T BE LIKE THAT.

ALL RIGHT, HOW DO I KNOW YOU WOULDN'T TELL ANYBODY MY PRIVATE STUFF?

PSYCHOLOGY TODAY

IT WOULD VIOLATE DOCTOR-PATIENT CONFIDENTIALITY.

69

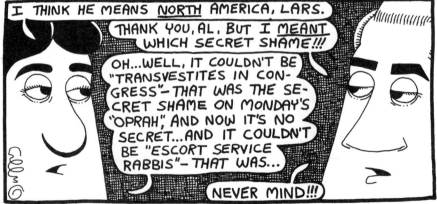

TALKING BACK TO THE TV IS NORMAL...

"THIS IS THE COMMERCIAL THE PHONE COMPANY DOESN'T WANT YOU TO SEE..."

THAT MAKES IT UNANIMOUS, PAL!!

TALKING BACK TO THE TOASTER IS A POSSIBLE INDICATION OF TROUBLE...

YOU CALL THIS "LIGHT"?!?

FOR A COMPLETE LIST OF APPLIANCE-RELATED CONVERSATIONAL DO'S AND DON'T'S, SEE YOUR DOCTOR.

WERE YOU A BOY SCOUT WHEN YOU WERE A BOY, AL?

THE COFFEE TABLE BOOK

I HAD MORE IMPORTANT THINGS ON MY MIND THAN TYING KNOTS WHEN I WAS A BOY, AXEL... I BELONGED TO A MORE SERIOUS ORGANIZATION...

WHICH ONE?

THE FLAT EARTH SOCIETY.

DO YOU THINK I'M TOO SHORT TO JOIN THE BOY SCOUTS, RÖLF?

YOUR HEIGHT IS FINE, YOUR WEIGHT IS FINE, YOUR SPECIES IS WRONG.

NORMALLY, AXEL, I WOULD HAVE TAKEN THE TIME TO LET YOU DOWN EASY, BUT GERALDO IS DOING A SHOW ON TOPLESS BANK TELLERS.

NO PROBLEM.

CLICK

YOU KNOW, RÖLF, FOR A LOT OF MEN I'VE DATED, THE PURSUIT OF WOMEN IS THEIR ENTIRE RAISON D'ÊTRE...

GEE, REALLY? I WOULD NEVER SAY THAT ABOUT MYSELF, MAXENE...

I HAVE A LOUSY FRENCH ACCENT.

WELL, THAT'S DEPRESSING... THE FIVE-DAY FORECAST PREDICTS 98 ON TUESDAY.

I CAN UNDERSTAND WHY YOU WOULD BE DEPRESSED, RÖLF, BUT PERSONALLY, I'M IMPRESSED THAT THEY WOULD ANNOUNCE YOUR BIRTHDAY ON TV, AND ALSO, IF I MAY ADD, YOU DON'T LOOK A DAY OVER 75.

HOW VERY DROLL.

IF THE HEAT IS BOTHERING YOU SO MUCH, RÖLF, WHY DON'T YOU GET AN OSCILLATING FAN?

I'LL HAVE YOU KNOW I'VE ALREADY GOT PLENTY OF FANS, AXEL, AND IF IT WEREN'T FOR THE FACT THAT THERE'S A MINOR IN THE HOUSE, I MIGHT INVITE A FEW OF THEM OVER...

AND BELIEVE ME, OSCILLATION WOULD NOT BE A PROBLEM!!

83

AH, SO _THAT'S_ BEEN THE PROBLEM AROUND HERE...

FAMILY

LET'S GO SIT IN THE KITCHEN, LANCE.

WHY, AXEL?

SAY IT WITH FLOWERS...

FAMILY CIRCLE

SAY IT WITH DISTANCE...

MISANTHROPY MONTHLY

DESERTED VACATION SPOTS

BECAUSE, ACCORDING TO THIS ARTICLE, AMERICANS ARE RETURNING TO THE KITCHEN AS THE CENTRAL GATHERING PLACE FOR MOVING FAMILY BONDING MOMENTS...

AND, OF COURSE, THE FAMILY THAT BONDS TOGETHER...

RESPONDS TOGETHER!!

WHO SAYS??

THE NATIONAL KITCHEN AND BATHROOM ASSOCIATION.

TRY DUNKING A STELLA DORO BREAD STICK IN YOUR SWISS MOCHA INTERNATIONAL COFFEE...IT'S _DEE-LISH!!_

JUST SO WE COVER ALL THE BASES, I THINK I'LL HAVE MINE IN THE BATHROOM.

92

WILL THERE BE ANYTHING ELSE TO-NIGHT?

ALL I CAN DO IS HOPE...

RÖLF, ARE YOU TRYING TO BE A JERK, OR WHAT?

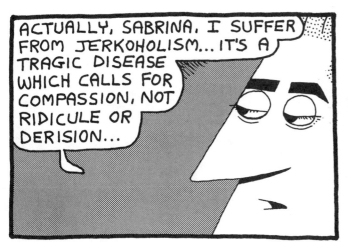

ACTUALLY, SABRINA, I SUFFER FROM JERKOHOLISM... IT'S A TRAGIC DISEASE WHICH CALLS FOR COMPASSION, NOT RIDICULE OR DERISION...

AS A MEMBER OF JERKOHOLICS ANONYMOUS, ALL I CAN DO IS TAKE IT ONE DATE AT A TIME....

I UNDERSTAND... THAT REMINDS ME—I JUST REMEMBERED I HAVE A D.O.J. SUPPORT GROUP MEETING TONIGHT...

LET ME GUESS... DATES OF JERKO-HOLICS?

BINGO.

STARTING TODAY ON THE FUSCO CHANNEL...

VENTRILOQUISM WEEK!

LANCE FUSCO AS...

"THE TEACHER"

AXEL FUSCO AS...

"THE STUDENT"

SCOTT MAGNUM AS...

"MR. JOHNSON"

CALL YOUR CABLE COMPANY NOW!

VARIETY

VENTRILOQUISM BOFFO AT BOX OFFICE!!

LANCE, WHEN ARE YOU GOING TO TEACH ME VENTRILOQUISM?

SOME OTHER TIME.

REJECTION IS SO MUCH EASIER TO TAKE FROM INANIMATE OBJECTS.

PLEASE, LANCE, PLEEEASE?!? WILL YOU TEACH ME THE NOBLE ART OF VENTRILOQUISM??

OKAY, AXEL...THE FIRST THING YOU NEED TO PRACTICE IS MAKING YOUR VOICE SOUND LIKE IT'S COMING FROM SOME-WHERE ELSE...

HOW DO I DO THAT??

WHY DON'T YOU GRAB THE NEXT BUS TO NEW YORK...THE HOLLAND TUNNEL HAS GREAT RESONANCE.

98

WOW, WHAT A HOT, HUMID DAY... I'M SWEATING LIKE JERRY LEWIS ON LABOR DAY!!

DO YOU EVER WEAR BERMUDAS DURING THE SUMMER, RÖLF?

GET READY TO LAUGH, FOLKS...

THE SHORTS OR THE ONIONS, RENÉE?

THE SHORTS!! WHY WOULD ANYBODY IN HIS RIGHT MIND WEAR BERMUDA ONIONS IN THE SUMMER?? OR ANY TIME?!? AND ANOTHER THING—WHY DO YOU KEEP MAKING THESE CRYPTIC LITTLE ASIDES TO NO ONE IN PARTICULAR?!?

DON'T YOU HATE IT WHEN YOUR DATE IS SO FAR OFF YOUR WAVELENGTH THAT YOUR BEST MATERIAL MAKES HER THINK YOU'RE PSYCHOTIC??

YEAH, LIKE THAT!! SEE?!?

SEE??

SEE?!!?

DON'T BE RIDICU-LOUS, AL—OUR PHONE IS <u>NOT</u> TAPPED! YOU'RE PARANOID!!

YOU KNOW THE OLD SAYING, LARS—"JUST BECAUSE I'M PAR-ANOID, IT DOESN'T MEAN I'M <u>NOT</u> BE-ING FOLLOWED!!"

LOOK—WE'LL BE HOME IN AN HOUR WITH A SOOTHING PEP-PERONI PIZZA... TURN ON THE TV AND TRY TO RELAX.

"THIS IS CBS..."

RÖLF, WHY DO YOU WEAR THE OCCASIONAL NECKTIE? WHAT'S THE OCCASION??

CLASSIFIED

HOPEFULLY, NO OCCASION, AXEL...I WEAR THEM WHEN I'M HAVING A PSYCHIC PREMONITION OF SOME KIND OF IMPEND-ING TRAGEDY WHERE A TIE IS REQUIRED...

YOU MEAN LIKE A FUNERAL?!!?

A FUNERAL...A WEDDING...A JOB INTERVIEW....

CLASSIFIED

WHAT DO YOU SAY WE GO OUT TONIGHT AND RUB SHOULDERS WITH SOME WOMEN, AL?

SOUNDS PRETTY UNORTHODOX, BUT I'LL GO GET READY.

FIVE MINUTES LATER

YOU CAN'T BE TOO CAREFUL IN THIS DAY AND AGE, LARS.

WHAT THE...?!?

SAFE SACKS.

57

YOUR EYES ARE LIKE TWO LIMPID POOLS, MY DEAR... WITH NARY A _HINT_ OF CHLORINE!

TELL ME, AL, DO YOU CONSIDER YOURSELF A LADIES' MAN?

HMM...I DON'T WANT TO COME OFF LIKE AN EGOMANIAC, YET I DON'T WANT TO SEEM INSECURE...

I DON'T WANT TO SOUND LIKE I'M BLOWING MY OWN HORN, YET I DON'T WANT IT TO SOUND LIKE MY HORN IS IN THE PAWN SHOP...

MAYBE I CAN DEFLECT THE QUESTION BY HIGHLIGHTING ONE OF MY STRONG POINTS, LIKE...LIKE...GIVING LADIES A LOT OF ROOM...

I GUESS YOU COULD SAY I'M A LADIES' ROOM MAN, RHONDA...

SO MUCH CAN HAPPEN TO AN IDEA BETWEEN THE SAFETY OF THE BRAIN AND THE DANGER OF THE LIPS.

LANCE, WHAT DO YOU SAY WE DRIVE DOWN TO THE SHORE FOR ONE LAST DAY AT THE BEACH BEFORE SUMMER IS OFFICIALLY HISTORY?

DON'T WORRY, AXEL— THE OZONE LAYER IS ABOUT TO RIP WIDE OPEN, AND THE THERMOSTAT ON THE GREENHOUSE EFFECT IS SET ALL THE WAY AT THE TOP...

IT'LL BE SUMMER FROM NOW ON.

ANY TIME YOU START GETTING ECOLOGICALLY AWARE, I KNOW IT'S MERELY A SMOKE SCREEN...

SMOKE SCREENS... THAT'S ANOTHER BIG PROBLEM.

IF YOU DON'T DRIVE ME, I'LL TAKE YOUR CAR.

I'VE GOT THE KEYS.

I'LL HITCH-HIKE.

WATCH OUT FOR THOSE PESKY SERIAL KILLERS.

I'LL TAKE A GREYHOUND.

THREATENING TO ELOPE DOESN'T FRIGHTEN ME EITHER, AXEL.

!!%?#©*!!

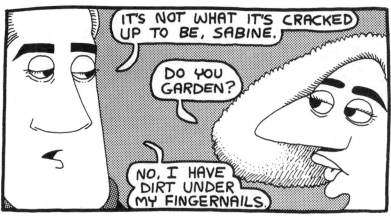

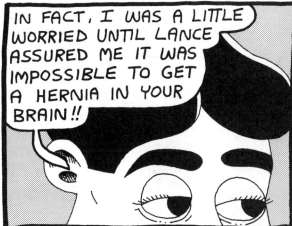

119

121

WELL, HERE IT IS—THE LEGENDARY FUSCO MANOR.

??? CLAP CLAP

I HAVE A FIRM POLICY OF NEVER CONTINUING A DATE WITH A MAN WHO HAS "THE CLAPPER" CONNECTED TO ANYTHING IN HIS HOUSE...

I'M ALSO TURNED OFF BY GINSU KNIVES, CHIA PETS, AND ANYTHING FOR PEOPLE WHO'VE FALLEN AND CAN'T GET UP.

YOU HAD ME DIS-ORIENTED THERE FOR A MINUTE, DAGMAR...

I'M NOT USED TO HEARING APPLAUSE OUTSIDE OF MY BEDROOM.

DO YOU HAVE ANY PLANS FOR THE WEEKEND, LANCE?

WE'RE THINKING ABOUT STAINING THE HOUSE.

STAINING THE HOUSE?? THE FUSCO BROTHERS??? I CAN'T PICTURE IT...

WE'RE CONSIDERING THROWING A WILD PARTY SATURDAY NIGHT...WE FIGURE THE HOUSE WILL BE PRETTY STAINED BY SUNDAY.

NOW I CAN PICTURE IT.

I TOLD GLORIA IT'S VERY HARD FOR A MAN TO COMMIT TO A WOMAN RIGHT UP UNTIL THE DAY HE DIES...

YEAH?

YOU KNOW—WHAT WITH ALL THE UNKNOWNS AND VARIABLES IN THIS WACKY WORLD...

YEAH?

SHE OFFERED TO CLEAR UP ONE OF THE UNKNOWNS AND VARIABLES FOR ME...

HOW?

BY PINPOINTING THE DAY I DIE.

YEAH, I REMEMBER WHEN MY LIFE WAS ON A ROLL, AXEL...

NOW, IT'S HARD TO GET STARTED ON A ROLL...I NEED ONE OF THOSE "EASY-START" ROLLS...THEY MAKE TOILET PAPER THAT WAY, WHY NOT LIFE???

FORGET ABOUT NOT BEING ON A ROLL, AL, AND START WORRYING ABOUT THE FACT THAT YOU'RE AT THE POINT WHERE YOU'RE ASKING A TEENAGE WOLVERINE WHY LIFE IS NOT LIKE TOILET PAPER.

NOW I'M FRIGHTENED.